CHEMISTRY IN THE KITCHEN

by Glen Phelan

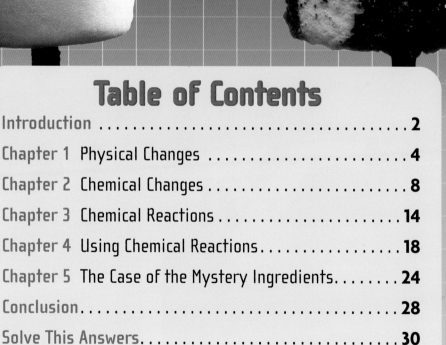

Table of Contents

INTRODUCTION

What things did you change this morning? You might think you didn't change anything. Maybe you woke up, made your bed, washed, got dressed, ate breakfast, took the bus to school, and went to the same classes as always. No changes, right?

Actually, each of those actions involved a number of changes. For example, when you made your bed, you changed the positions of the sheet, blanket, and pillow. When you washed, you changed your body by removing oils and dirt. You changed the bar of soap by mixing it with water. Now think again about how you might have changed things in the last few hours.

▲ What changes are happening here?

▲ Exposure to the air and water makes wood rot.

Changes happen all the time. Just look outside. Puddles of rainwater evaporate into the air. Seeds grow to be tall trees. Wind and water break rocks into tiny bits. All of those changes happen naturally.

Sometimes we want to control how things change. For instance, you can add fertilizer to the soil to make vegetables grow faster and bigger. We can slow down or stop some changes, too. For example, you can paint a wooden fence to keep it from rotting.

There's one place in your home where people control changes the most. It's the kitchen! What changes are happening there? You're about to find out.

PHYSICAL CHANGES

Do you ever make salad? You might chop lettuce, cut tomatoes, or slice cucumbers. Maybe you put it all in a bowl, add some dressing, and mix it all up. With each bite, you can still taste the lettuce, tomatoes, cucumbers, and dressing. That's because each ingredient is still the same kind of food. Each ingredient is still the same kind of **matter**. Matter is anything that has mass and takes up space.

Chopping and slicing change the shape and size of each kind of food. You change a physical **property**, or characteristic, of the matter. As a result, a physical change occurs. In a physical change, the appearance or form of matter changes, but it is still the same kind of matter.

▲ This lettuce looks different than the head of lettuce, but it is still lettuce.

Gaining Heat

Changing the size or shape of matter is one way to change it physically. Another way is to add heat to it.

Do you ever help make crispy rice treats? You drop the marshmallows into a pan on the stove. Then you turn on the stove to low heat. After a couple of minutes, the marshmallows begin to melt. That's because they gain heat energy. This added heat causes the marshmallow **molecules** to move faster. As the molecules begin to slip and slide past one another, the solid marshmallows become a gooey liquid, but it is still marshmallow. One lick of the spoon will tell you that.

It's a Fact

Marshmallows were once made from the mallow plant. It grew—where else?—in marshes!

▲ When a substance melts, it goes through a physical change.

"PhhhWEEEEEE . . ." What's that rising, ear-piercing whistle? The liquid water in the kettle is boiling. It's turning into a gas called water **vapor**. You can't pour the vapor into a glass, but it's the same matter as the water you drink.

LOSING HEAT

Melting and boiling are physical changes. Both occur when matter gains heat. But what happens when matter loses heat? Different kinds of physical changes occur.

When you fill an ice-cube tray and put it in the freezer, heat moves from the liquid water into the cold air of the freezer. The liquid's molecules move slower and slower. They vibrate slowly in place until they form a rigid pattern. That's when the liquid freezes.

1. SOLVE THIS

Water freezes at 32°F (0°C). Adding salt to water lowers the freezing point to 0°F (-18°C). Salt is spread on icy streets at noon when the temperature is 21°F (-6°C). The ice melts. At 6 P.M. the melted ice refreezes. How did the air temperature change between noon and 6 P.M.?

MATH ✓ POINT
Does your answer make sense? Why or why not?

When water vapor meets cooler air, the vapor loses heat energy. The water molecules slow down. The water changes back to tiny drops of liquid. We say the water vapor **condenses**. The drops are so tiny that they float in the air as a cloud of steam.

You might have seen bigger drops of condensation on the inside lid of a pot of boiling water. The drops let you know that another physical change has occurred.

▲ Steam is condensed water vapor.

⚗ HANDS-ON EXPERIMENT
SEPARATE SALT WATER

A physical change happens when you mix salt with water. Can you separate this matter into its original ingredients?

What You'll Need
salt, cup of water, teaspoon, dish

What To Do
1. Observe the salt. Look at the shape and size of the salt crystals. Feel them.
2. Mix a teaspoon of salt into a cup of water. Stir until the salt is dissolved.
3. Pour a few teaspoons of salt water into the dish. Let the dish sit for a couple of hours. Then observe the contents of the dish.

What Do You Think?
1. What is left in the dish after a couple of hours?
2. What happened to the water?
3. What kind of change did the salt water go through?

CHEMICAL CHANGES

You may be getting the idea that there's a lot of chemistry in cooking. You're right. You can think of the kitchen as a laboratory. But hold on—our discoveries in kitchen chemistry are just beginning.

THE CHEMISTRY OF BREAKFAST

What kind of change happens when you make pancakes? You add milk and eggs to some pancake mix.

You pour the stirred batter onto a hot surface. Soon little bubbles appear. With one or two flips, your liquid batter becomes a solid pancake.

What happened to the ingredients? They have undergone a chemical change. In a chemical change, matter forms new substances. The new substances have properties that are different from the original ingredients.

▲ Pancakes taste different than their ingredients of milk, eggs, and powdered mix. That's because the cooked pancake is a different substance.

The chemical change that resulted in pancakes occurred because the pancake mixture gained heat energy. That happens a lot when cooking. Think about boiling an egg. The boiling of the water is a physical change. But if you place a raw egg in the hot water, chemical changes happen inside the egg. First, tiny strands of protein begin to uncoil. With more heat energy, the ends of the straightened protein strands join with other protein strands. The water around each strand is forced out. The raw, liquid egg becomes a solid, hard-boiled egg.

▲ Chemical changes turn a raw egg into a hard-boiled egg.

 POINT

Picture It

Draw a series of step-by-step sketches showing how to prepare your favorite cooked food. Then write a caption that describes a chemical change that occurs.

A CHANGE WITHOUT HEAT

Adding heat is one way to cause chemical changes, but it's not the only way.

Did you ever bite into an apple and then set it aside for a few minutes? The white part of the apple turns brown. A chemical change has occurred. Chemicals in the apple combine with oxygen in the air. A new type of matter forms. It has properties that are different from those of the original apple. One of these properties is color—brown. Other changed properties are taste and texture. The apple is no longer sweet and crunchy.

Varieties of Apples Grown in Washington

Red Delicious	37%
Gala	15%
Fuji	14%
Golden Delicious	13%
Granny Smith	12%
Braeburn	3%
Cripps Pink	2%
Jonagold	1%
Cameo	1%
Other	2%

◀ The apple combines with oxygen in the air to turn brown—a chemical change.

2. SOLVE THIS

Use the chart above to answer these questions. If the state of Washington harvested 100 million boxes of apples in a year, how many boxes of Red Delicious apples were harvested? How many of Granny Smith? How many of Braeburn?

MATH ✓ POINT   How can you check your answers?

HANDS-ON EXPERIMENT

Stop the Chemical Change

How can you protect apple slices from going through a chemical change?

What You'll Need

2 apples, quartered; bowl; water; paper plate

What To Do

1. Place four apple quarters in a bowl. Add water to the bowl until all the slices are covered.
2. Place the other four apple quarters on a paper plate.
3. Wait 30 minutes. Observe the apple quarters from the plate and the water.

What Do You Think?

What differences did you observe in the apples? What caused these differences?

MORE OXYGEN CHANGES

Oxygen causes chemical changes in all sorts of matter—not just food. Take iron, for example. Iron is a solid metal. When iron is exposed to moist air, a chemical change occurs. The iron combines slowly with oxygen in the air. A new kind of matter forms. It's reddish and brittle. Do you know what this matter is called? It's rust.

Do you have any copper-bottomed pans in your kitchen? Chances are, they're not as bright and shiny as they used to be. Copper is another metal that combines with oxygen. This chemical change forms a dull coating. The coating is not copper. It's a new kind of substance called copper oxide. The same thing happens to pennies.

▲ A chemical change with oxygen turns the iron in this car to rust.

⸮ HANDS-ON EXPERIMENT

Homemade Copper Cleaner

You can buy powders, pastes, and liquids to remove copper oxide from a surface. Maybe you can do the same job without these chemicals. Let's see.

What You'll Need

dull pennies, plastic cup, lemon juice, plastic spoon, paper towels

What To Do

1. Place the pennies in a cup. Pour lemon juice over the pennies until they are covered.
2. Wait 10 minutes. Use a spoon to remove the pennies from the cup. Place the pennies on a paper towel.
3. Rub each penny with another paper towel. Observe what happens.

What Do You Think?

Did the pennies change after being placed in the lemon juice? How? What does this tell you about copper oxide and lemon juice?

It's a Fact

- The penny is made up of 97.5% zinc and 2.5% copper.
- There may be over 130 billion pennies in circulation today.
- The average penny lasts twenty-five years.
- The U.S. Mint produces about thirty million pennies a day.

13

CHEMICAL REACTIONS

How does a chemical change happen? To answer that, we have to take a closer look at matter.

All matter is made up of **atoms**. Sometimes the atoms of one substance interact with the atoms of another substance. The atoms rearrange and form something new. This rearrangement of atoms is a **chemical reaction**. Each original substance is a **reactant**. The new matter that forms is a **product**.

CHEMICAL SHORTHAND

Remember the chemical change that made the copper-bottomed pans dull? You can describe the chemical reaction that caused this change by saying, "Two atoms of copper react with two atoms of oxygen to form two molecules of copper oxide."

ACTIVITY

Pour a little vinegar into a clear, plastic cup. Then add about half a teaspoonful of baking soda to the vinegar. Stir. Do you think a chemical reaction is taking place? How do you know?

That's a mouthful! Is there a shorter, easier way to describe this reaction? There is.

A **chemical equation** is a shorthand way to describe a chemical reaction. Instead of words, a chemical equation uses symbols and formulas. Look at the chemical equation below. Match each symbol with the words that describe the reaction that takes place.

The reactants in this chemical reaction are copper (Cu) and oxygen (O). The product is copper oxide. The plus sign shows that copper and oxygen are reacting. The arrow means "forms" or "produces."

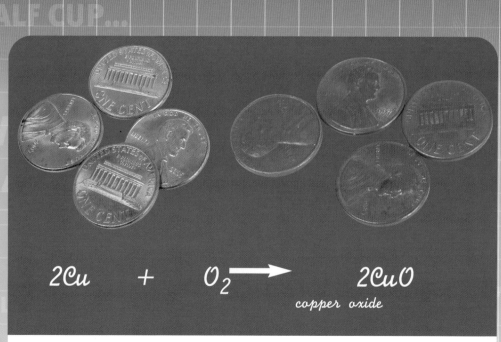

$$2Cu \quad + \quad O_2 \longrightarrow \quad 2CuO$$
copper oxide

▲ This chemical equation shows that copper reacts with oxygen to form copper oxide.

BALANCED EQUATIONS

Different chemical reactions have different reactants and products. But all chemical reactions are alike in one way. The total number of atoms in the reactants always equals the total number of atoms in the products. In other words, the equation is balanced.

In addition, the type of atoms in the reactants is always the same as the type of atoms in the products. That's because matter is not created or destroyed during a chemical reaction. It is simply rearranged.

3. SOLVE THIS

Suppose you have the following coins: 5 pennies, 6 nickels, 4 dimes, and 3 quarters.

- Use circles of paper to represent the coins. Write the value of one coin in each circle. Place the coins into two groups. Add up the value in each group. Then total the value of both groups.

- Now rearrange the coins to make two different groups. Again, add up the value in each group and the total value of both groups.

a. What changed between the first two groups and the second two groups of coins?

b. What stayed the same between the first two groups and the second two groups?

c. How does this activity model chemical reactions?

MATH ☑ POINT   What steps did you follow to solve the problem?

▲ The brown crust on the marshmallow shows a chemical reaction.

CLUES OF A CHEMICAL REACTION

During a chemical reaction, you cannot actually see atoms rearranging. So how do you know a reaction is occurring? There are all sorts of clues. If you did the activity on page 14, you noticed a lot of fizzing. Bubbles of carbon dioxide gas formed when you mixed the vinegar and baking soda.

Little bubbles also appear in pancake batter when it is heated.

The production of a gas is one sign of a chemical reaction. Other signs include heat, light, smoke, odors, and color changes. What clues are shown in the picture on this page?

USING CHEMICAL REACTIONS

Chemical reactions happen all around you. Some of these reactions happen slowly. Days may pass before milk turns sour. Months may pass before rust forms on iron. Millions of years may pass before the remains of plants become coal and oil.

Other reactions happen very quickly. Paper placed in a fire turns to ash and smoke in seconds. Clothing stains wash away as soon as detergent and dirt begin to mix. Washing your hands with warm, soapy water quickly removes unseen germs from your skin.

How fast or slow a chemical reaction occurs is called its **reaction rate**. Temperature affects reaction rate. When reactants gain heat energy, they interact more rapidly.

▲ Chemical reactions make a banana ripen, then over-ripen, over several days.

SURFACE AREA AND REACTION RATE

Surface area also affects reaction rate. Surface area is the total amount of space each side of an object takes up. Increasing the surface area of a reactant gives the substance more opportunity to mix with other substances. The reaction happens faster that way.

So how do you increase the surface area of an object? Break it up!

For example, if you heat a sugar cube, a chemical reaction produces caramel. The sugar will melt and cook faster if you break the cube into smaller pieces.

▲ Sugar turns into caramel when heated.

4. SOLVE THIS

A gelatin cube is 4 inches (10 centimeters) long and 4 inches (10 centimeters) wide. If the cube is cut in half, does the total surface area increase, decrease, or remain the same? By how much?

MATH ☑ POINT How can you check your work?

19

MAKING BREAD

Did you ever wonder why most bread has to rise before being baked? Have you ever noticed holes in a slice of bread? It's all about chemical reactions.

Most of the bread you eat is made in three major steps:

1. making the dough
2. letting the dough rise
3. baking the risen dough

You begin by mixing ingredients, such as flour, milk, butter, sugar, and eggs. This makes bread dough. Can you bake it right away? You could, but the bread would be very heavy and dense.

To make the bread lighter, you have to "fluff it up," or make it rise. So you add a very special ingredient—a leavening agent. A leavening agent is a substance that produces bubbles of carbon dioxide gas. These bubbles move through the dough and expand it, or make it rise. They give the bread a light, fluffy texture. Three commonly used leavening agents are baking soda, baking powder, and yeast.

It's a Fact

Yeast is a living organism. One gram of yeast may contain about 25 billion cells!

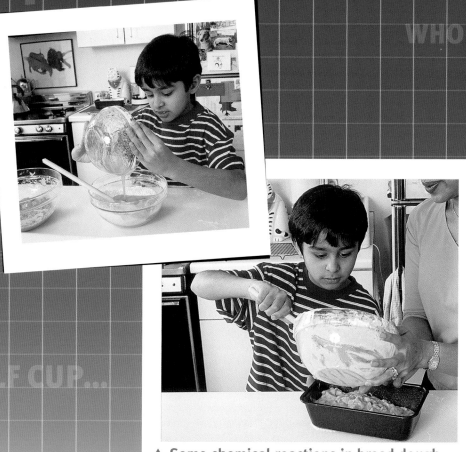

▲ Some chemical reactions in bread dough begin as soon as the ingredients are mixed.

5. SOLVE THIS

People who live in high-altitude locations such as Denver, Colorado, often must adjust their recipes. This is true for bread recipes. At high elevations, carbon dioxide gas produced by leavening agents expands more. Bakers generally reduce the amount of yeast in a recipe by 20%. If a recipe calls for 1 ounce (28 grams) of dry yeast, how much will a baker at a high elevation use?

MATH ☑ POINT What steps did you follow to find your answer?

21

⚲ HANDS-ON EXPERIMENT
Observing the Action of Yeast

What goes on inside a loaf of bread when yeast mixes with sugar? Hint: Yeast changes sugar into carbon dioxide and ethanol.

What You'll Need

1 packet of active dry yeast	large rubber balloon
1 cup of very warm water	1-liter plastic bottle
2 tablespoons of sugar	spoon

What To Do

1. Stretch the balloon. Then blow into it and release the air a few times to stretch it out more.
2. Place the sugar and yeast in the cup of warm water. Stir.
3. Pour the mixture into the bottle. Stretch the end of the balloon around the bottle's top. Observe what happens.

What Do You Think?

1. How did the balloon change?
2. Would this change have happened without the sugar? Explain why.

SLOWING DOWN A CHEMICAL REACTION

Why do you put milk in the refrigerator? The main reason is to slow down chemical reactions.

Milk is made safe to drink at a dairy farm. But it always has some germs in it, especially after you open it and expose it to the air. These organisms grow and eventually produce chemical reactions that spoil the milk.

In the refrigerator, heat energy from the milk moves into the cool air. The milk gets cooler. This coolness slows down the growth and action of the germs, so the milk stays fresh for many days.

▲ Why do some foods need to be refrigerated?

THEY MADE A DIFFERENCE

In the early 1860s, a French winemaker found that something was causing his wines to become bitter. The winemaker asked chemist Louis Pasteur to study the problem. Pasteur knew yeast was used to make wine. He soon discovered that other tiny microorganisms could damage the wine. Pasteur developed a way of using heat to kill these harmful microorganisms. His method, called pasteurization, is used today to keep milk and other beverages safe to drink.

THE CASE OF THE MYSTERY INGREDIENTS

You've decided to bake some bread for your family. You go to the cabinet to get your ingredients. Instead of labeled packages, you find three containers with no labels. Each container holds a white powder. The flour, baking soda, and sugar all look the same to you. How can you tell them apart? You can use what you know about chemical reactions!

The powders might look alike, but each substance contains a specific combination of atoms. Each group of atoms reacts differently when mixed with other substances. You can use this fact to identify the ingredients. First, you need to determine just how flour, baking soda, and sugar react to two liquids—vinegar and iodine solution. Follow these experiments to learn how you can tell your ingredients apart!

▲ How can you tell these substances apart?

⚗ HANDS-ON EXPERIMENT
Looking for a Reaction

What You'll Need

flour	vinegar
baking soda	iodine solution
sugar	2 eyedroppers
magnifying glass	6 paper plates

What To Do

1. Put a small amount of flour on each of two paper plates. Use the magnifying glass to look carefully at the flour. Describe how it looks. Rub some flour between your fingers. Describe how it feels.

2. Add one drop of vinegar to one plate. Observe what happens.

3. Add one drop of iodine solution to the other plate. (Be careful with the iodine. It stains.) Observe what happens.

4. Repeat steps 1 to 3 with baking soda and then with sugar.

What Do You Think?

How could you use your results to test the mystery ingredients?

⸮ HANDS-ON EXPERIMENT
Let's Make Some Bread

Would you like to see matter change before your very eyes? All you have to do is follow this recipe for Irish soda bread. As you follow the steps, think about whether your actions are causing a physical change or a chemical change. Be sure an adult helps you with your baking.

What You'll Need

mixing bowl

large spoon

3 cups whole wheat flour

1 cup all-purpose flour

3/4 teaspoon double-acting
baking powder

1 teaspoon baking soda

1 tablespoon salt

1 2/3 cups buttermilk

cake pan

butter or margarine

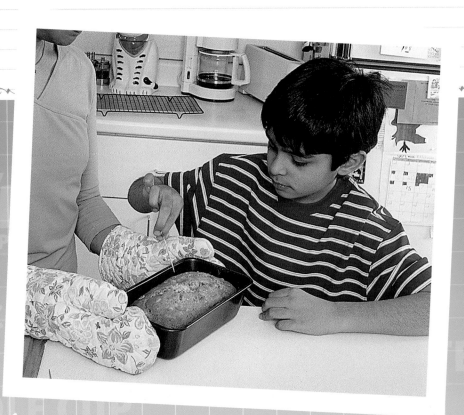

What You'll Do

1. Preheat the oven to 375°F.
2. Rub butter or margarine all around the inside of a bread or cake pan.
3. Combine all the ingredients except the buttermilk in a bowl. Mix thoroughly.
4. Add the buttermilk and mix further.
5. Knead the dough on a lightly floured surface for about three minutes.
6. Shape the dough into a round loaf and put in the pan. Place the pan in the preheated oven and bake for 35 to 40 minutes.
7. Let the loaf cool for several minutes. Enjoy your bread!

CAREERS
Food Chemist

Food chemists are scientists who study the chemical composition of foods. They use this information to develop new types of food products. Food chemists should be curious people who enjoy science and are good at solving problems.

CONCLUSION

Matter is constantly changing. Cutting, melting, freezing, and boiling cause matter to change physically. These processes do not produce new kinds of matter.

Sometimes matter changes to form a new substance with properties that are different from the original substances. This type of change is a chemical change. Iron turning to rust and milk turning sour are types of chemical changes.

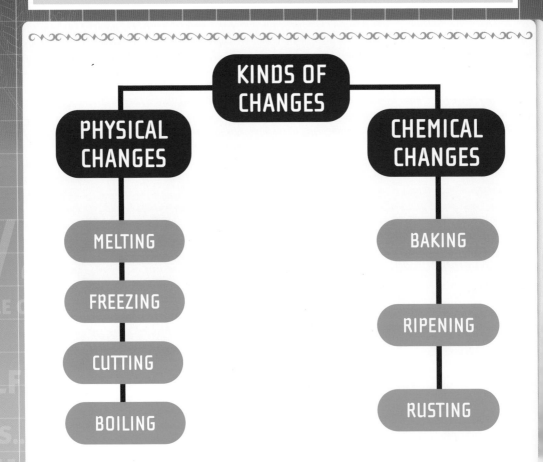

KINDS OF CHANGES

PHYSICAL CHANGES

CHEMICAL CHANGES

MELTING

FREEZING

CUTTING

BOILING

BAKING

RIPENING

RUSTING

Chemical changes happen when the atoms of substances interact. This interaction is called a chemical reaction. A chemical equation is a way of representing what occurs in a chemical reaction.

We use our knowledge of chemical reactions to store and prepare foods. When we store foods in a refrigerator, we are slowing down chemical reactions that could make the foods unsafe to eat. When we heat foods, we are speeding up chemical reactions that make foods tasty.

You probably never thought of the kitchen as a laboratory. But from cooking to cleaning to storing, the kitchen is the perfect place to see chemistry in action.

 POINT

Make Connections

Think back to the chemical reactions you read about in this book. Which ones have you already observed? Which ones would you like to make happen?

29

1. Page 6
The temperature dropped at least 21°F (12°C).

2. Page 10
a. Red Delicious: 37% of 100,000,000 = 37 million, or 37,000,000
b. Granny Smith: 12% of 100,000,000 = 12 million, or 12,000,000
c. Braeburn: 3% of 100,000,000 = 3 million, or 3,000,000

3. Page 16
a. The arrangement of coins was different.
b. The total number of coins, the types of coins, and their total value were the same.
c. In a chemical reaction, the reactants are rearranged, but they are not created or destroyed.

4. Page 19
Cutting the cube in half will increase its surface area.
The total surface area of the original cube is
16 square inches (in.^{2}) x 6 faces = 96 in.^{2}.
The total surface area of the cut cubes is
8 in.^{2} x 8 faces + 16 in.^{2} x 4 faces =
64 in.^{2} + 64 in.^{2} = 128 in.^{2}.
(100 square centimeters [cm^2] x 6 faces = 600 cm^2.
The total surface area of the cut cubes is
50 cm^2 x 8 faces + 100cm^2 x 4 faces = 800 cm^2.)

5. Page 21
20% of 1 ounce = .2 ounce (20% of 28 grams = 5.6 grams)
1 ounce – .2 ounce = .8 ounce (28 grams – 5.6 grams = 22.4 grams)

GLOSSARY

atom   (A-tum) the smallest particle of a chemical element that has all the properties of that element (page 14)

chemical equation   (KEH-mih-kul ih-KWAY-zhun) letters and symbols and formulas that represent the elements and compounds that take part in a chemical reaction (page 15)

chemical reaction   (KEH-mih-kul ree-AK-shun) when atoms of different substances interact to form new and different substances (page 14)

condense   (kun-DENS) to change from a gas to a liquid (page 7)

matter   (MA-ter) anything that has mass and takes up space (page 4)

molecule   (MAH-leh-kyool) the smallest particle of a substance that still has the properties of that substance and is made of two or more atoms (page 5)

product   (PRAH-dukt) matter produced as a result of a chemical reaction (page 14)

property   (PRAH-per-tee) a characteristic of something (page 4)

reactant   (ree-AK-tunt) a substance that interacts with another type of matter in a chemical reaction (page 14)

reaction rate   (ree-AK-shun RATE) rate at which a chemical reaction occurs (page 18)

surface area   (SER-fus AIR-ee-uh) total amount of space each side of an object takes up (page 19)

vapor   (VAY-per) water in the form of a gas (page 6)

INDEX